The Fantastical Collection of Enlightening Short Stories

or

A Place Called Earth

by

David Kentish

The Fantastical Collection of Enlightening Short Stories,

© 2021 by David Kentish.

For information contact

david.j.kentish@gmail.com

or visit the website

https://david-kentish.square.site

This edition replaces the original «A Place Called Earth» of 2014.

Contents

vi

PROLOGUE

Whilst travelling from Western Australia across to Queensland in 2010 on a caravan trip, I gained some insight for this story whilst driving.

Several situations presented themselves to me and from that insight, these short stories developed over a period of time.

After completing several of the stories, I had one of our fellow campers, who was a schoolteacher, read them and give me some indication of the stories' value and readability. His comments were very encouraging so I continued with the rest of the chapters as time went by.

Having been brought up in a Christian household, I have a fair knowledge of the Bible. I also have a reasonable knowledge of science-based theory on how things began and developed in our little section of the galaxy. So, I have combined many aspects of the two theories to make up these stories and put them down in print in my own fashion.

Recently I had the opportunity to complete the stories and present them in a book so that others might gain some enlightenment and entertainment from them.

I hope that you find my slant on the theory of evolution entertaining.

viii

HOW IT ALL STARTED

Sometime after the "Big Bang", which was followed by a long period of time for everything to settle, Mother Nature began to carry out her plan for the planet that came to be known as Earth.

This plan would take many, many millennia to accomplish and sometimes she would make the odd miscalculation that would need to be rectified.

The first thing that needed to be done was to stop Earth from spinning so fast. It was spinning so fast, in fact, that every time she put something on the surface of Earth, it would fly off so quickly that she could not catch it and it would get lost, way out in space.

But the surface of Earth was so hot that it hurt her hands when she applied them to the surface of Earth to slow it down.

The solution was so simple! She'd need something to cool her hands.

So, Mother Nature just went off, found a few comets that were flying around, collected them all together and came back with the ice. By holding the ice in her hands and then gripping Earth between them, she was able to slow it down without hurting her hands and at the same time the surface of Earth was cooled. Some of this ice stayed on the surface of Earth. In fact, it is still there to this day. Some is at the top of Earth and some is at the bottom of Earth so this proves that this story is accurate.

Now that Earth is spinning at the correct rate, she began to put things onto the surface. These things were like land and water.

She was not too sure just how to arrange these things because she had not done this type of work previously. So, she just stood back and threw some land at the surface and it stuck there.

Next she threw some water at Earth and it stuck there too!

How amazing!

But Mother Nature reckoned that she still had two major problems.

All of the land was in one big lump, spread over a large area.

The water that she had thrown onto the surface of Earth had turned salty and covered most of the surface of Earth, so she called this, Sea.

While she was sorting out how she was going to rectify these problems she decided that the land looked very bare and brown.

Mother Nature has a wonderful garden and she selected from this, many different plants to spread around the land which she had just put on Earth. These she planted. What she needed now was some water for the plants.

Mother Nature needed someone to help her, so she created a friend who is known as Weather. Now she got Weather to blow up a wind over the water. This wind collected some moisture that was rising from the surface of the sea and when the wind blew over the land this moisture turned into rain. This rain fell on the land and soon the plants which she had planted began to grow.

One of the problems for Mother Nature arose here. She had asked Weather to blow up some wind to create the rain but she forgot to tell Weather that she could stop after a while. Not too many years later the plants had grown to an enormous size. Not only did they grow tall but some of them also grew out all over the land and now she couldn't walk around Earth because there were just so many plants.

While she was thinking on this problem, she called on Weather to have a break from the wind and rain and let the sunshine for a while. Well, this was marvellous because now with the extra warmth the plants grew even faster and very soon the whole of the land was covered in a jungle.

"Oh! What to do", exclaimed Mother Nature.

Then it came to her! "I know! I'll make Seasons so that there will be some time for rain, that can be winter and some time for sun, which could be summer. That should help the plants to grow at just about the right rate so they won't take over everything.

The Seasons worked well but the trees and things just kept on growing.

Then Mother Nature noticed that some of the older plants became so old and so big that they died. Soon other plants would take over their space but she was not completely happy with this.

"The jungle looks so green, and it's the same shade of green. I'd like to see some different colours", Mother Nature exclaimed to herself.

So, Mother Nature in her wisdom put flowers onto the plants. Not just the same flowers but different flowers. In fact, there were so many different flowers that every different type of plant had its own flower.

After a while Mother Nature stood back and admired her work.

"Well, that does look a picture!" she said as she congratulated herself.

There were red flowers, yellow flowers, white flowers, orange flowers, pink flowers, green flowers and even a few blue flowers just to keep things on a balance. She was pleased with her efforts to make the jungle look prettier. Not only prettier, now the plants could re-produce and make more of themselves when they became too old or too big and died.

Now that Mother Nature was happy that she had this situation under control, she thought that she would tackle another of the problems. And that was to sort out this problem of all of the land being in one place.

With there being so much rain in the past, many rivers had formed and now some of the rainwater was being washed back into the sea. These rivers cut deep cracks in the surface of the land and this gave Mother Nature an idea.

"If I cut through this land in a few places, I could separate the pieces and scatter them all over the surface of Earth instead of just in one place." So, she did.

She pushed pieces of land in all directions. One of the pieces became northern America, some became southern America. Another piece became Africa. Another piece became Europe and another became Asia. There were several other pieces lying around so she just gave them a bit of a shove to send them on their way. One of these pieces was India.

Now, Mother Nature didn't really know her own strength, she must have pushed too hard because India collided with Asia and got stuck. Not only did it get stuck but it collided at a fast rate of speed and the end result was that when it hit, it kept going for a while and pushed up a great range of mountains. These are called the Himalayas.

Another of these pieces of land ended up near the bottom of Earth. It was out of her sight for such a long time that she forgot all about it.

There were lots of little bits left over so she scattered these all around and they came to form the islands which we see all over the surface of Earth.

Now that there were pieces of land all over the surface of Earth, Mother Nature needed to tackle the problem of the plants which had grown so many and so large and totally covered the lands of Earth. But one good thing to come of all these plants was that now Earth has an atmosphere. There was lots of oxygen. There were some other gasses in the atmosphere as well but these were only minor and were mostly good gasses anyway.

Knowing that in her own garden, there were things which ate her plants, she didn't want these same things eating the plants on Earth because there soon would not be any plants. Some of those garden bugs were not very nice anyway, she thought.

So, she put some plant eating dinosaurs onto Earth. These are known as herbivores and are very good at eating plants.

After many millennia had past, Mother Nature noticed that in fact the herbivore dinosaurs had eaten more of the plants than she wanted. She could see great bare patches where there were no longer plants. And she was not happy.

How to overcome this problem? She asked herself.

Mother Nature put onto the lands of Earth some meat-eating dinosaurs. They are known as carnivores and would help to control things by eating some of the plant eating dinosaurs and therefore reducing the number of plants which were being consumed. After many millions of years, there developed a happy balance of meat eaters controlling the plant eaters, which were controlling the plants.

She was happy with all she had done. Now with Weather doing her job, Seasons doing her work and the dinosaurs doing their work, it was a happy place of everything in balance. The plants are now reproducing, and they looked so good with their pretty flowers, too!

But disaster is about to strike.

Way out in space and travelling at a very fast speed is a giant piece of rock called a meteor. This piece of rock has been travelling around out in space since the Big Bang happened and has not hit anything in all of that time. Of course, Mother Nature knew of this meteor being out there but since it hasn't hit anything so far, she thought that her Earth should be safe from a collision.

Little did she know but that is just what was about to happen.

One day just as Sunrise was happening; she saw this big rock heading straight towards Earth. She was horrified because a big meteor like that could really make a mess of all the good work she had done. She tried to stop it but it was just too large and going too fast for her efforts to have any effect on its path.

She tried to warn the dinosaurs and the plants but they just couldn't do anything in the short time they had before the meteor collided with Earth.

Across the morning sky she could see this massive thing flying through the atmosphere which was created by the plants. There was a long tail coming from behind the meteor and she could see lumps of rock in the tail too.

Bang!

The meteor crashed into Earth and hit the ocean just near the land.

It made such a loud bang that she thought that it would be nearly as loud as that big one which happened so long ago.

The meteor was very hot and it dried up a lot of oceans, making most of it into steam which rose in large clouds to block out some of the sun. It made such a large hole in the land that it vaporised the land into dust and massive clouds of this dust also flew up into the air blocking out the rest of the light from Sun.

Now all of Earth was dark. Even darker than Night and this lasted for a long time.

Many, many years it lasted.

Because of the dark, Mother Nature could not see anything. She could not find out if anything needed her help. Even if she could find out if anything needed her help she didn't know what she could do anyway.

She was not very happy. She was distraught. Mother Nature was totally devastated.

But although things lasted like this for a very long time, she eventually began to see a glimmer of light. She noticed that the sea was rising and getting close to its former level. She noticed that the land was brown but there were no plants left. She noticed that there were no dinosaurs left, they were all dead too. They had either starved from lack of food or were poisoned from the dust in the atmosphere. It did not look too good to Mother Nature and she was depressed.

As the light from Sun slowly became brighter over the many years that it took for the atmosphere to clear, she thought that she could do something in the oceans to help.

Because there was now enough water, she decided to put some water animals into the oceans of Earth. These she called fish.

Now, Mother Nature had learned a very valuable lesson when she introduced dinosaurs to the lands of Earth so she made sure that she had included herbivorous as well as a balance of carnivorous fish. This would keep the balance correct in the oceans of Earth. And she was happy with the way this worked out.

Now the fish of the oceans were becoming more and more adapted to their home, she brought in some special ones that she liked very much. Some of these were the dolphins and the whales. She just liked the way they did things and now that the air was breathable again they did very well living in the oceans of Earth and breathing the air, while all the other fish were getting their oxygen through the water with their gills.

After the fish of the oceans of Earth had been around for many years, Mother Nature thought about some more animals for the lands of Earth. You see, the plants of Earth had regenerated from seeds which were buried deep in the ground. There were not many plants yet but there were becoming more of them all the time. She didn't want to put in those large animals like the dinosaurs again because they were just too hard to handle and made so much mess, so she put onto the lands of Earth lots of different animals. She found some animals which liked the colder climates nearer to the top and bottom of Earth, like polar bears and penguins. She found some animals which liked the heat and moisture of the tropics, like elephants and monkeys. She found some animals which liked the dry of the inland like kangaroos and geckos and she found some animals which liked to be close to the oceans of Earth, like sea eagles.

Many of the animals were herbivores and many were carnivores so they should be able to keep a balance and keep Earth a happy place for all to live.

This plan worked very well.

Earth was recovering from the devastation which was caused by that meteor.

For several millennia, Mother Nature was satisfied that her plan was in fact great. She was happy again.

The plants were flourishing again, their flowers keeping her happy. The animals fitted in together despite the odd argument, the fish of the oceans were doing very well in their home and it looked like the balance was just about perfect.

But Mother Nature could foresee a problem and she took a lot of time to consider how she was going to overcome this problem.

Although the animals of the lands of Earth and the fish of the oceans of Earth are all doing well, there just seemed to be something missing and it took a while for her to work out what it was that was missing.

She could appreciate all of the good things about the plants with their flowers and the pleasant way which the plants covered the lands of Earth. She could appreciate all of the animals of the lands of Earth and their many and varied colours and habits. She could appreciate all of the fish of the oceans of Earth but she thought that she should be able to share this great appreciation with someone else.

Then she thought of man.

Yes, she thought, I'll put man in there, so he too can appreciate all of the good things which are in the oceans of Earth and on the lands of Earth. He can harvest some of the plants for his food and there are some of the animals which he will be able to hunt and have for his food. So, with this in mind, Mother Nature introduced man to a special place on one of the lands of Earth.

Mother Nature set man down in an area where vegetable and animal food was abundant. She gave him a mate and together they prospered in The Land of Plenty. Soon there were many of man and their mates. They continued to multiply just as the animals did when they were first introduced onto the lands of Earth.

She watched them for many, many years to learn about them and try to come to understand them, so she that could help man to get the best benefit from the lands of Earth and the oceans of Earth.

So, Mother Nature just watched and learnt all about man.

It was not a long time until man's activity on the land was starting to show as he took from the land and did not replace what he had taken, so Mother Nature showed man how to grow crops so he could sustain himself and his family. This was successful.

Soon man had outgrown the lands of Earth which Mother Nature had set aside for him, so he began wandering far from The Land of Plenty. Some of man wandered to the east and settled at the east of the land known as Asia. Some of man wandered to the north into where it was much colder, where for part of the year the land was still covered in snow and ice. Some of man wandered to the west of the land and settled in the west coast of the land known as Africa. Some of man wandered to the south and into the southern parts of the land known as southern Africa.

This movement of man across this land of Earth was very acceptable to Mother Nature because now the pressure on the land was spread over a greater area.

Man flourished as did the animals and plants of the lands of Earth. Man, also began to use the oceans of Earth to gather fish for his food.

Mother Nature was happy that this was a good balance and everything was good with Earth.

So, at this time, when everything was good, Mother Nature took some time out for herself and entered into a slumber for many years.

After several thousand years Mother Nature awoke from her restful slumber just to see how her plan for this favourite place of hers, called Earth, was progressing.

Well, she certainly was in for a shock.

Those of man who had stayed in the land of plenty had totally destroyed it. There was just sand everywhere. The plants and trees had all gone. There was just this barren waste with rolling bare hills which she called a desert.

She immediately called on Weather to get her to send in some winds to blow more moisture onto the lands which have been devastated. But Weather could not get the winds to carry moisture into the desert because the winds just dried out before they could reach that far and all she could do was just create a massive dust storm. As soon as Weather could see what was happening she got the winds to stop blowing so fiercely so as to not do any more damage.

It seems that some mountains between the desert and the ocean was helping to stop the wind bringing in the rain, so Mother Nature created an Earthquake and reduced the mountains to hills but this was just not enough to put rain into all of the parts of the desert.

Still there is a desert where The Land of Plenty used to be and now part of it is called Sahara.

Mother Nature was very upset with man for doing this to her favourite place on the lands of Earth. She was so angry that she began to tremble. She was trembling so much that the lands on which she was standing began to shake. Then all of the lands of Earth began to shake as Mother Nature's anger continued.

Some of the lands of Earth began to move and in the gaps where they had moved from, unusual events began occurring. The hot molten lava which lay just beneath the surface of the lands of Earth and the oceans of Earth began to spew out of the ground. This red-hot lava began to form new mountains as the lands tried to protect themselves from becoming damaged but the lava continued to flow out of so many places in all of the lands of Earth. This lava flowing from out of the ground of the lands of

Earth was known as volcanoes. Some of these were located under the oceans of Earth as well, so the entire Earth was going through change again.

Unfortunately, with these volcanoes erupting all over Earth, the sun was almost blotted out. The sky became darkened and Mother Nature stopped her trembling from her anger and began to calm herself so she didn't do damage to her Earth.

She almost created a catastrophe.

Presently most of the volcanoes stopped erupting and settled down to become dormant. After a while they became safe and soon after that, man returned to the burnt-out lands and began life there again.

But not all of the volcanoes stopped erupting. There were still a few on the lands of Earth and in the oceans of Earth which continued to erupt from time to time. Even today there are still a few of these volcanoes erupting. These are there as a reminder to everyone that Mother Nature can have a very bad temper if she is badly annoyed. So, we need to be careful not to arouse her anger.

Since the time of the volcanoes, man has learnt some new skills. He began to build boats which allow him to travel over the oceans of Earth. Now man can trade his wares across all of the oceans of Earth and also he can reach all of the lands of Earth that are separated by the oceans of Earth.

This is good.

This is good because man can now shift to where he can make a new start. The Americas open up for man for the first time. All of those islands which Mother Nature created so long ago can now have man visit or stay on them. With his new boats, man can travel everywhere. The land at the bottom of Earth known as Australia had man visit it and many of them stayed to become the first Australians. Mother Nature had forgotten this piece of land with its diverse climates but was now happy that some of man were there to spend some time and appreciate it too.

Over the millennia, man has always found an excuse to harm his fellow man. Sometimes this is done one man to another but mostly this is done by one kingdom to another. The king or ruler of that area has become greedy and that greed can only be met by taking more land. This is what causes these conflicts known as wars. Some wars are short and the problem resolved quickly but some time these wars have been known to last for a thousand years. This has killed many of man of the lands of Earth.

Man started doing these wars on foot. Then as he tamed the animals, he would fight the wars while riding on the back of these animals. Soon he began to use boats to conduct wars and now these wars can spread all over the oceans and the lands of Earth.

Mother Nature is distressed by what she sees man doing here and has great difficulty in understanding why man is doing these things. But for most of man, life is peaceful.

Man has become so many, that in places Mother Nature has found it difficult to balance the greed of man and the needs of man to feed himself.

Some places just will not support the numbers which man has grown to and she has great difficulty in sending man to different places so that he can find or grow enough food for himself.

Man continues to feed off the animals which Mother Nature has provided and he also is able to grow many crops for himself to use. Man, also has learned to farm some special animals and now he can produce nearly all of his needs.

But Mother Nature is still teaching man how to look after the lands of Earth and the oceans of Earth.

So, soon she hopes that these little difficulties will be corrected and then the plants, the animals, the birds, the fishes and man can live in harmony in this place which Mother Nature has taken such a long, loving time to create.

A place called Earth.

WHO OWNS THE SUNSET?

The plan for the place called Earth has been put together by Mother Nature. She has been helped by Sun, Moon, Daytime and Night-time. The plan has been working well for many millennia. This divided the days into segments which would allow all of Earth to fit in together. This plan works well.

Sunset follows Daytime and is shown before Night-time. Sunrise follows Night-time is shown before Daytime. This divides the days into periods of darkness and periods of lightness.

You see, there are those animals and birds which like to hunt for their food during the day. These animals and birds are called diurnals and they tend to rest or sleep during the night, because their most active time is during the day. So, in order for these animals and birds to get their rest, the plan allowed for them to have plenty of time during the night for that rest, so that they would be refreshed the next morning, be active and feed throughout the next day.

There is a group of animals and birds who prefer to do their hunting at night and these animals and birds are called nocturnal. The nocturnal animals and birds spend a lot of the night being active and feeding and by the end of night they would like to rest so that they too can be ready for another night's feeding and activity the following night.

One day, the question was posed; who owns the Sunset?

The Daytime decided that he owned the sunset.

So, to prove his point he spent all day talking to the diurnal animals and birds who agreed with him to put their names to a list which Daytime would present to Night-time, who reckoned that she owned the sunset. He thought that if he could produce a longer list than Night-time, he would win the argument.

Not to be out-done Night-time decided that if Day-time was going to those lengths to prove that he owned the sunset, she also would spend all of the night encouraging all of the nocturnal animals and birds to put their names to her list so that she could present this to Day-time to show that it was in fact She who owned the sunset.

Now, this had been going on for some time and it was approaching the time when each list was to be presented by Daytime and Night-time to each other so one of them could prove that in fact it was he or she who owned the sunset.

There were two long lists. Each of them had been very busy in getting all of the animals and birds to put their names to the list.

On Night-times list were animals like the kangaroo and there were many different varieties of kangaroos; eastern reds, western reds, greys, rock, tree, just to name a few. There were a lot of wallabies. And as for bats! Well, you never saw such a long list of all the different types of bats that had put their name to Night-times list. There were quolls, geckos, rabbits, bandicoots, foxes, bilbies, frogs, possums and dingoes. In fact, the list of nocturnal animals was very extensive.

To add to this list of course are the nocturnal birds: Owls, nightjars, tawny frogmouths, penguins and so on.

There were a lot who didn't get their names on the list. All of the nocturnal insects missed out because Night-time thought that with just the animals and birds there would have been more than enough to complete her list and convince Daytime that she owned the Sunset.

Of course, Daytime's list also had a lot of names on it. On this list were also the kangaroos, thylacines, wallabies, foxes, dingoes because these animals are also present and active in the bush during parts of the day as well. So now we have them on both lists. But there are also snakes, lizards, crocodiles, buffalos, Tasmanian devils, tortoises, rats and goannas.

Daytime's birds list was, however, far more extensive than Night-times list of birds. Here we see listed are brolga, swans, emus, ducks, penguins, bustards, crows, robins, kites, honeyeaters, falcons, wrens, magpies, kookaburras just to name a portion of the total number of birds which appeared on Daytime's list.

Now, it is approaching time to present the lists to each other but there is a big problem.

Daytime and Night-time just can't seem to arrange a time when both of them can be together to compare lists. This is because, you see, they are separated by the sunset in the evening and the sunrise in the morning. No matter what they tried to do, they just could not find a time when they could get together.

This is a real problem and they begin to argue about this problem as well as the main issue of "who owned the Sunset". And the arguing continued for a very long time. It was getting to the situation where many of the animals and birds had had enough of this bickering. They were totally fed up with this continuous arguing which was going on between Daytime and Night-time as to who owned the sunset.

In fact, with all of this arguing, the bush became so noisy that Mother Nature was aroused from her long slumber.

Things have been so peaceful for such a long time that it took a while for her to understand the cause of all of this arguing and noise. She talked with Nigh-time and she talked with Daytime to see if she could find out the cause of the noise.

She could see that Daytime has some value to his argument but she could also see the value to the argument presented by Night-time.

So, the bickering and arguing continued, while Mother Nature pondered on the problem of who owns the Sunset.

Then to make matters worse along came man.

Now in the afternoons after a long day hunting to bring in food for his family in the cave, man would relax and sit back and watch the sunset. Man's mate, woman, who spent most of her day cleaning the cave, looking after the children, fetching the water, collecting the fruit and digging the yams would sit with man to view the sunset. The view of the sunset helped them to relax after their hard day's work.

They could hear all of the arguing about which of Daytime or Night-time owns the sunset and it pained them to hear this because the sunset was so beautiful some days.

Then along comes Weather to add her opinion to the argument. Well, she said, if you two don't stop arguing shortly and sort out this problem, I'll soon steer the clouds away from the west so that there will never be a pretty sunset for you to see.

Well, this certainly increased the debate now it seemed that everyone was in on the argument.

While Daytime and Night-time claimed ownership of the sunset, everyone else seemed to be of the opinion that because they all enjoyed looking at the sunset that in fact they should own it.

Well now, this was becoming simply too much for Mother Nature. She was thinking that it was up to her to solve this problem of who owns the sunset. After some time, she had a plan in mind which she would present to everyone but there was this problem of getting them together.

So, Mother Nature created an eclipse of the Moon. This was a total eclipse and the land was nearly as dark as if it were night.

Now this caused all of the diurnals and the nocturnals to be disoriented but they could spend some time together. Even Daytime and Night-time were present.

Mother Nature tells them in no uncertain terms that it is she who controls the sunset.

No-one owns the sunset, she said.

The sunset is there to mark the end of day and the beginning of night.

She went on to explain how she had control of Weather and she would sometimes ask Weather to send some clouds to the west to be near the sunset so it would create those very pretty colours. Sometimes she decided that there would be no clouds near the sunset so that everyone could have a greater appreciation of the colourful sunset when she did get Weather to send in some clouds.

Everyone from the animals, birds, bugs, fishes and man could be satisfied that Mother Nature had control of things and was happy to present them with a sunset every day and from time to time with a splendid sunset.

A sunset that everyone can enjoy.

Daytime, Night-time and Weather were disappointed because they didn't win their argument but they all agreed that this was a good outcome, as they all could do what they do, when they do it and not have to worry about who owns the sunset.

It seemed that with Mother Nature taking care of things, there will be sunsets for everyone to appreciate and enjoy.

Now everyone throughout the land is happy.

I'M MORE IMPORTANT THAN YOU.

Now many centuries after the ownership of the sunset has been finalised and everyone was happy with Mother Nature's decision, Sunset and Sunrise had a discussion.

The Sunrise said, "I'm more important than you, Sunset, because I herald in the new day. It gives everyone the chance to start off the new day with confidence."

The Sunset claimed, "But if that's all you do then I don't have anything to worry about because, you see, I close off the day and bring in the night. It gives everybody the chance to rest from their day's labours and enjoy a pretty sunset.

"But I have some very brilliant sunrises too!" claimed Sunrise.

This started out as just a bit of fun but soon the fun turned to bickering and then into an argument.

Sunrise claimed that he was the most important but Sunset thought that she was the most important.

They argued for another century or so and with each decade the argument became more vigorous. They both still kept to their original claims and added in some more details, trying to convince the other that they were the more important.

Animals' ancestors told them of a time long, long ago when there was an argument about who owns the sunset. There are a lot more animals around now so there were more for Sunset's and Sunrise's argument to affect.

Animals said to both Sunset and Sunrise, "We know you are both important to us every day and we really appreciated your pleasant shows which you put on for us but please can we stop this arguing?" they pleaded.

Not to be left silent, the birds also told Sunset and Sunrise that they too were fed up with this argument, telling them that the bush was getting far too noisy with all of this argumentation going on.

But this had very little effect on how Sunset and Sunrise carried on. They still wanted to argue because each of them still thought that they were the more important.

Sun put forward a suggestion which he thought would help Sunset and Sunrise to sort out their differences. "Well," he said, "If I withdrew my services, then neither of you would be very good. How can you have a sunset or a sunrise without me? How about you let me be the most important and you two stop this nonsense."

The next thing we know, Moon comes along and puts forward her thoughts. "I agree with Sun's comments. But you know that Sunrise separates the night from the morning and that Sunset creates the break between day and night, so why don't you both be satisfied that you both do a great job and both are very important to us all."

All of the animals and the birds agreed with Moon's comments. They thought that she had explained how they felt too!

Sunset and Sunrise took these suggestions to heart and for another century the argument died down.

But there was always that little bickering going on between Sunset and Sunrise.

"I'm more important than you." They said to each other whenever they had the opportunity.

Like all arguments which are not settled this one raged again.

Both Sunset and Sunrise were adamant that they were the more important and nothing which Sun or Moon or Animals or Birds said would make any difference.

The numbers of Man had increased by this time and they occupied most of the land.

Those of Man who lived on the east coast could see the Sunrise over the ocean, while those of Man who lived on the west coast could see the Sunset over the ocean. Now while this situation caused a few comments between the west coast man and the east coast man, they did not argue. Both the Sunrise and Sunset held a special place in their hearts. They enjoyed the very colourful display which was put on for their benefit nearly every day.

The argument between Sunset and Sunrise became noisy again.

By this time, everyone had told both Sunset and Sunrise how they felt about this argument and the noise which they created while having this argument but it made little difference. They both kept up their tirade for decades. It was becoming louder and louder as they, each of them, kept on at the other about how one was more important than the other.

Again Sun, Moon, Animals, Birds and Man told Sunset and Sunrise to stop this terrible argument and noise, but they continued on. Increasingly everyone was getting to the stage when they thought that it would be better not to have a sunset or a sunrise if they had to put up with all of this discomfort and noise.

To sort out the problem, Sun called Moon, Animals, Birds and Man together to see if they could work out a solution for these two arguers.

Animals said, "Our ancestors told us of a time many centuries ago when there was an argument about the ownership of the sunset and they had Mother Nature help them sort out the problem. Perhaps we need to call her and see if she can help us this time too!"

So, Sun, being the oldest, called on Mother Nature and told her of this problem with the argument between Sunset and Sunrise and the noise that they were making. Mother Nature responded by saying that she would be happy to help as she had done previously.

Because both Sunset and Sunrise were at opposite ends of the day, she decided that the only way they could come together was to display another eclipse of the moon.

This eclipse caused the day to become so short that both Sunrise and Sunset could be present.

When Mother Nature had their attention, this is what she said to them. "Many, many years ago, there was an argument about who owned the Sunset. After I had told those involved all about Weather and how I had suggested that no-one actually owns the Sunset, the problem was resolved. Now you two need to understand what the others think of your lack of respect for their wishes. They all want to experience both Sunset at the end of day and Sunrise at the end of night. It gives everyone a sense of timing. Time to start the day, or time to finish the day. Now without either one of you, they would not be able to appreciate that time of day. So, I really think that you both need to consider that you are neither important nor unimportant to everyone who looks at you."

She sent them away to think about what she had told them and said that she would talk to each one individually in a short time to see what they have learned from this experience.

Sunset and Sunrise went away and presently the eclipse ended and it was daylight again. And quiet.

A decade passed and one day Mother Nature was watching as Sunrise made a magnificent display, one of the best for many years, in fact. Now Sunrise, she said, that was a magnificent display which you just put on for everyone, what do you think made such a pretty sight?

Sunrise replied, Well Mother Nature, since you told us about how we should respect the wishes of the others, I got to thinking that it was the way which I would like them to treat me. So now I don't argue with Sunset anymore, I feel I can do a very good job of separating night from day and give everyone some peace of mind and that everything is great.

After day was finished, Mother Nature spoke to Sunset after she had provided a great display with so many colours in the sky at that special time. She asked the same question. Now, Sunset she said, that was a magnificent display which you just put on for everyone, what do you think made such a pretty sight?

Mother Nature, said Sunset, I have treated everyone badly and for that I am truly sorry. I would not like to be treated the way that I have treated them, so I reckon that I'll just spend my time at the same time every day doing what I can to make everyone happy, that I can provide them with a sense of time and occasionally a brilliant sunset.

Mother Nature, Animals, Birds, Man, Moon and Sun were very happy that the argument had been resolved.

Now everyone can live in peace again and enjoy the beautiful Sunrises and Sunsets as well as the quiet time between them both.

30

Everyone is happy once more and Mother Nature is pleased.

THE DAY SUNRISE WAS LATE

A very, very long time ago Sun, Moon, Mother Nature, Daytime, Night-time, Sunrise and Sunset devised a plan that would give equal time to day and night.

Here are some of the many reasons for this plan.

You see, there are those animals and birds which like to hunt for their food during the day. These animals and birds are called diurnals and they tend to rest or sleep during the night, because their most active time is during the day. So, in order for these animals and birds to get their rest, the plan allowed for them to have plenty of time during the night for that rest, so that they would be refreshed the next morning, be active and feed throughout the next day.

There is a group of animals and birds who prefer to do their hunting at night and these animals and birds are called nocturnal. The nocturnal animals and birds spend a lot of the night being active and feeding and by the end of night they would like to rest so that they too can be ready for another night's feeding and activity the following night.

Now, so that the diurnals would know when it's time to wake up from their rest, the plan allowed for sunrise to happen at the beginning of day, so that they did not miss any of their active or feeding time.

Also included in this plan is a sunset which not only marks the end of the diurnal's active time but also the beginning of the time when the nocturnals would become active.

So, with day and night separated by sunset and sunrise, all of the nocturnal and diurnal animals and birds are able to work their active time to their best advantage. They can also work out their best rest time.

At different times of the year, the nights would become longer and the days shorter. This allowed the land to warm up during the day and remain warmer during the night. Another time of the year, the nights would become longer and the days shorter, so that Weather could organise some rain to fall.

This plan was developed over many years and when Sun, Moon, Sunrise, Sunset, Daytime, Night-time, Animals and Birds were happy with the few adjustments which were needed, everyone was happy.

The diurnals were very happy because they knew that they could wait for the sunrise before they needed to get out of bed. Likewise, the nocturnals could wait for the sunset till they had to get out of bed.

About this time Man came to the land. He too was mostly diurnal but some of Man were also nocturnal. So, they fitted into the plan along with Birds and Animals who were either nocturnal or diurnal.

But who tells Sunrise to get ready?

Who tells Sunset to get ready?

Well, you see, Night-time has told Sunrise that when it started to lose its darkness, Sunrise should get ready to follow this lightening of the darkness across the land so that all of the animals and birds could get their sunrise at the correct time. This was fine for Sunrise but he had to race right across the land and cover that entire distance in just three hours.

Boy that was fast!

That was very fast, because Sunrise had to run at about one thousand kilometres per hour so that he could get from the east coast to the west coast in that three hours' time period.

When Sunrise reached the west coast he could have a rest before he needed to start his return journey to the east coast so that he could be there in time for when Night-time next began to lose its darkness and he must go to work again.

But Sunset had the same problem.

As day became darker towards its end, Sunset had to get ready so that she should put on her display right across the land so that Night-time could follow.

Every time that either Sunset or Sunrise returned to the east coast after having put on their display, they tried to travel by a different route so they could see different things on the land as they returned.

Now, one day when Sunrise had reached the west coast he was extremely tired and instead of just resting he fell into a sound sleep. When he woke up, Sunset had finished and it was very dark. So, he headed off to the east coast by the shortest route that he knew of. This should make up for the lost time while he was asleep.

But this time of the year was very wet. There had been a lot of rain and many of the rivers and creeks had flowed and right in the middle of the land was this extremely big waterhole. It covered so much of the land that Sunrise could not find a way around it. Now he was going to be late when Night-time began to lose its darkness and he was supposed to go to work.

Sunrise had to travel a long way to the north so that he could get around the massive lake of water. He was going to be very late.

He didn't know how his being late in the morning was going to affect all of the nocturnals and diurnals activities.

He just didn't know.

Unknown to Sunrise, Man in his wisdom, had selected this very day to begin daylight saving on the east coast. Not knowing this, he pressed on and nearly got to the east coast as Night-time began to lose its darkness.

Some of Man, who lived near the east coast were not too sure if they should advance or retard their clocks to meet the new time that was known as daylight saving. However, most of them advanced their clocks and were correct. They would be seeing the night as it loses its darkness and were at work or fetching their food before Sunrise had a chance to begin his job.

Night-time had lost nearly all of its darkness by the time that Sunrise arrived. He was quite late.

The nocturnals were angry with Sunrise; their rest time had to be reduced by the same amount as his lateness.

The diurnals were angry with Sunrise because now they had less time for the gathering of food and their other activities.

Night-time was not happy with Sunrise because he was late and she had to wait for him before she lost all of her darkness.

Day was not happy with Sunrise because he couldn't start showing his daylight until after Sunrise had finished.

It was a mess!

Everyone was out of step with the day!

The diurnals continued with their daytime activities but needed to work faster so that they could get all of their things done that they needed to do before the day began losing its light and Sunset appeared.

But Sunset was on time that day for everyone except those of Man who lived near the east coast and altered their clocks for daylight saving. Many of them went to bed before Sunset could complete her display.

Although Man who lived near the east coast's clock did not agree with Sunset, she raced across the land as she had done before. The Sunset which she displayed when she arrived at the west coast was a magnificent one and all of Man who lived near the west coast was pleased to see such a great sunset after such a bad start to the day.

As Sunset moved in her westerly direction, she passed Sunrise who was on his way back to the east coast. She scorned him for his tardiness at being late that morning and suggested that he didn't do it again as she could not help him if or when he was late.

After a few days, everyone got back on track with the plan which had been set up by Sun, Moon, Mother Nature, Daytime, Night-time, Sunrise and Sunset.

Since Mans arrival, he too fitted in well with the plan. This was so, possibly with the exception of east coast Man who had changed his clocks to daylight saving.

Sunrise was never late again!

He always returned to the east coast just as soon as he had finished his display at the west coast and Daytime began. He would rest near the east coast so he was waiting for Night-time to lose her darkness and he could again begin his display.

Everyone was happy.

MOON

At about the time when Mother Nature was slowing down Earth she also spent some time working on another problem.

She was to work on a number of problems while she was working on her project of Earth and this one was no less important than any of them.

Another small planet-like object had been attracted to Earth. This planetlet would travel around Earth and sometimes could be seen from the surface of Earth. It had a much uncoordinated path and sometimes it would come dangerously close to the surface of Earth and Mother Nature was getting anxious that it might collide with Earth and cause a catastrophe.

So that Mother Nature could keep a track of this little planet she decided that she would call it Moon.

Moon was made of different stuff to Earth as they had come from different places when the "BIG BANG" happened which created them. While Earth had a hot centre and a solid mantle, Moon was just warm and the cold surface was covered with a deep, smooth, grey, powder-like substance with a few rocks.

The path which Moon took in the beginning was very erratic. Sometimes it was above the top of Earth and sometimes it was below the bottom of Earth but Moon spent most of its time above the middle or the equator of Earth.

Moon was also travelling at different speeds. Sometimes it could be seen two or three times a day as it raced around Earth while at other times it would slow down and not be seen for several days.

Mother Nature was not very happy with this arrangement so while she was arranging the details on Earth she also took some time to work out ways that she could fix the problem with Moon.

After she had spent some time working on her project on Earth and she had got it to rotate at the speed of 365.25 times each year she thought that Moon should rotate around earth at least each 28 days so that would make it 13 times each year.

As she had already sorted out the different season for Earth, this worked in well with those plans as now Moon would rotate Earth about 3.25 times for each season. This would give Moon sufficient time to do what she had planned for it to do.

While she was working on her project of Earth she was watching Moon to see how this new speed was working.

While she was happy with the way the speed of Moon was going, she was still apprehensive of the fact that Moon was still too close to Earth and that a small miscalculation could cause a collision and therefore disaster. Disaster is what Mother Nature most wanted to avoid.

Mother Nature reduced the amount of gravity which Moon had, so that it would move away from Earth. After a few adjustments with the amount of gravity of Moon she settled for a gravity of just one fifth of that of Earth. This was just about right most of the time.

With Moon rotating around Earth at a different speed to Earth, sometimes it could be seen at night. Sometimes it was present in the day but mostly it could not be seen at this time.

Sometimes Earth would come between Moon and Sun and this would make Moon look like it had a piece missing. It didn't really, it just looked like that because Earth caused a shadow to fall on the surface of Moon, so that bit in the shadow could not be seen. This is called an ECLIPSE OF THE EARTH.

What was happening here was Moon was like a big reflector. It would reflect some of the light from Sun to Earth. Mother Nature did it this way so that there would be some light during Night-time so that the plants and nocturnal animals would be able to see if only just a little bit. This plan is working well.

During Day-time Sun would provide all the light that was necessary for the things which needed light on Earth so with Moon providing some light at Night-time this was a good balance.

Because of the different rates of rotation of Moon and Earth, sometimes Moon would be above a Day-time part of Earth. If the Moon comes between Sun and Earth during the day it can cause a shadow to appear on the surface of Earth. This is called an ECLIPSE OF THE MOON.

Mother Nature uses ways where she can change a few of these things from time to time if she needs to.

There are always a few pieces of rock flying through space and some of these have hit Earth and caused a few minor problems. Mother Nature was not happy with her Earth being hit by these objects.

After watching this happen a few times, she decided on a course of action which would work for a short time but it failed in the long term.

When some of the larger rocks approached Earth she would move Moon so that the pieces of rock would hit Moon instead of Earth. Because of the powdery surface, Moon as able to absorb the shock of the impact much better than Earth. If you look at Moon now with a telescope you can see where these collisions have occurred.

The big problem with this practice is that these pieces of rock which fly through space are so uncoordinated that Mother Nature has no way of knowing just when they will come or from which direction until the last few minutes. She was able to move Moon many times to intersect the pieces of rock but there were several times when it wasn't possible for her to do that. She was very sorry that some of these got through her protection. One large piece of rock in particular caused a lot of harm to her Earth.

While Mother Nature was watching the relationship with Earth and Moon she noticed that Moon was affecting the tides of the oceans on Earth.

Although she had sorted out the relative gravities of both Earth and Moon to keep them separated, they do move closer at times and then move away again.

Like the seasons on Earth, Moon also has seasons and these are called "PHASES".

When Moon is full in the Night-time sky and shining brightly, she called this FULL MOON. When Moon was in the shadow of Earth and could not be seen, this is called NEW MOON. So, Moon would wax and wane between full and new. Between these two phases of Moon are ones like FIRST QUARTER and LAST QUARTER when Moon looked like it would hold water or not hold water.

When Moon is in its full phase, it comes closer to Earth and would appear much larger than at other times. When this occurred, the effect that Moon has on the tides of the oceans of Earth was greater. When Moon was above an area the tides would be full and other areas would be experiencing low tides. The opposite of this was also true as Moon rotated around Earth.

With Moon rotating around Earth each 28 days many of the inhabitants of Earth used this as a cycle for their own benefit. There will be a discussion about this at a later time.

With Moon and Earth performing together as she has set out, after the few adjustments which she has done, Mother Nature is happy with the way things are working together.

At this time, she takes some time out for herself and has a rest.

THE LAND NEAR THE BOTTOM OF EARTH.

Mother Nature had done a marvellous job of putting her plan together for the place she called Earth.

She enjoyed looking at what she has developed. She stood back and looked at the large round globe which was the planet Earth and then looking even closer, she could see all of those things which she had put there to make her planet complete. She had the salty oceans of Earth, where she put all of the fish. There were the large pieces of the lands of Earth where she had put all of the plants and animals. There were the islands which came from all of the pieces of the lands of Earth that didn't fit anywhere else.

And there is that piece of land which she pushed away so long ago and forgot about. She had pushed this piece of land away from that big mass of land which she divided up so many years ago and sent it on its way, without much direction. It had bounced off several other pieces of land on its journey and ended up near the bottom of earth and stuck there. It had been stuck there for several millennia before she remembered that piece of land near the bottom of Earth.

When it finished hitting all of the other pieces of land and completed its journey, it stopped just below the underside of the equator. The equator is that part of Earth that is midway between the top of Earth and the bottom of Earth. If you were to travel around Earth that would be the longest place that you could travel in a straight line. The equator is also that part of Earth that gets the most light and heat from Sun.

So, this piece of land enjoys a lot of light and heat from Sun in its northern parts, which make it hot. Some of the parts which are further south get less heat and light and this makes it warm. Because this piece of land near the bottom of Earth is surrounded by the oceans of Earth, it gets a lot more rain near the edge of the land than it does in the middle of the land. This causes a lot more of Mother Nature's trees and other vegetation to grow and prosper closer the edge of the land near the oceans of Earth than those areas which are nearer to the middle of the land near the bottom of Earth.

The edge of this land is green and abundant with life while the area at the middle of the land near the bottom of Earth is hot and dry and some places are desert.

While this land was on the move, after Mother Nature pushed it on its way, some parts of it went under the waters of the oceans of Earth and became inundated with this salty sea water. By the time this land near the bottom of Earth had stopped moving, it was all well above the levels of the waters in the oceans. That is with the exception of the centre of it which is still below the level of the water of the oceans of Earth.

In the lowest parts there is still a lot of salt that is left over from the time when it was under the sea. There are many other places on this land where there are still some puddles of salty water.

Mostly these salty puddles are dry because not very much rain can reach them but just sometimes these salty puddles do have some water in them.

Mother Nature has asked Weather to blow up some winds over the oceans of Earth to cause some more rain to fall over the middle parts of this land but Weather is only able to do this sometimes. Weather finds it very, very difficult to get enough rain to fall in the middle of this land near the bottom of Earth. She has to cause some larger amounts of rain to fall in some close by areas so that the water from this rain will flow into the low areas near the middle of the land near the bottom of Earth. This heavy rainfall has caused many rivers to be formed which flow into the middle of the land. But even these rivers are not able to take all of the water which Weather provides for the middle of the land. This extra water must spill out over the edges of the rivers and spread over a wide area before it can reach the middle of the land near the bottom of Earth. This spreading out of the water is called floods.

These floods which spread out so far from the rivers make some plants grow all over the land. These plants which Mother Nature has developed just for this particular reason grow very quickly when there is a flood. Just a few days after the flood has past, there are many new plants poking their flowers up to look at Sun.

Because these plants are here after the floods, there are animals which Mother Nature has trained to live off this very harsh environment. Some of these animals are very different from those which Mother Nature has developed for other lands of Earth.

Back in the time when dinosaurs roamed the lands of Earth and some of them in the oceans of Earth, there were some of them on this land near the bottom of Earth as well. Some of these dinosaurs used to inhabit part of the land near the bottom of Earth and some of the aquatic dinosaurs would inhabit the sea that was close to the middle of the land near the bottom of Earth. Unfortunately, these aquatic dinosaurs disappeared when the land near the bottom of Earth rose up and the inland sea drained away. This happened just before that big meteor hit Earth and caused the catastrophe that wiped out all of the dinosaurs of the lands of Earth.

When Mother Nature put the new animals onto Earth after the big catastrophe had cleared away, she put some animals down here on the land near the bottom of Earth as well.

Because Mother Nature had forgotten all about this land near the bottom of Earth for so long, she thought that she should do something special with the animals for this land near the bottom of Earth.

They had to be able to survive in this unusual climate of droughts and flooding rains, of hot dry winds and in some places even snow. She had such a variety of these new animals that she would only put the special ones at each place that were suited to that area.

She thought that her special animals should be seen here and nowhere else on earth so she developed some which we know as marsupials.

The marsupials have a pouch at the front of their belly where the young ones can stay until they can feed and defend for themselves. When Mother Nature found out how well these new animals of hers worked out, she developed more animals with the pouch, as this design fitted in so well. She developed different marsupials for the different regions so they would fit in best.

She developed animals that we know of as Koalas, Wombats, Kangaroos, Wallabies, Wallaroos, Possums, Gliders, Devils (*of Tasmania*), Quolls, Numbats, Bandicoots and Bilbies and spread these all over the land near the bottom of Earth.

But it wasn't just marsupials that she had developed for this special place on Earth. There also were crocodiles, skinks, goannas, snakes, thylacines, bats, and even worms.

There were also birds of so many colours that they are like the colours of the rainbow. Here we can still see her parrots, honeyeaters, owls, kites, eagles, swallows, seagulls, penguins, pelicans and Willie wagtails.

She also made some birds that didn't fly and this is what we know as the Emu.

She also put onto the land near the bottom of Earth some very large animals. These survived for many years and were known as mega-fauna. Some of them were nearly as large as the dinosaurs which were on the lands of Earth previously. Some of these looked like giant kangaroos, while some others looked like giant goannas. Some even looked like enormous koalas.

When she had finished settling in her special animals onto the land near the bottom of Earth she had a rest and sat back relaxing while she watched her new animals enjoy their life on the land near the bottom of Earth. She enjoyed watching them so much and it was so relaxing that she fell asleep.

While she was asleep some of man who had learnt to use boats on the seas of Earth had visited the land near the bottom of Earth and stayed there to live. At first there was not many of them but after a lot of years their numbers became many and they had spread all over the land near the bottom of Earth. They would move around and take their food that Mother Nature had provided and when this food was all gone they would move on to another area. They kept on moving all over the land near the bottom of Earth.

All of Mother Nature's mega-fauna were slow in moving and this made them very easy to catch. They did make such good tucker for this man but soon man had eaten so many, there were none left.

When Mother Nature woke up from her sleep and saw what this man had done to her special animals on the land near the bottom of Earth, she became angry. She was very angry because of all the special effort she had gone to, to put such special animals here onto the land near the bottom of Earth. Now they were all gone and never to be seen again.

To display her anger, she turned the skin of this new man of the land near the bottom of Earth a dark colour so she could recognise them for ever more.

She allowed this man with the dark skin to stay in her land near the bottom of Earth but he had to live off the other animals which were able to move much faster. So now he had to become a bit smarter and run a lot faster to be able to catch his food. His mate, woman with the dark skin, would collect the seeds of trees and dig in the ground for the yams and roots which Mother Nature had provided for them.

Some of the other lands of Earth, where man had lighter skin, had become full of man and now that he had boats he could move around on the oceans of Earth to other lands of Earth. Some of them came to the land near the bottom of Earth.

Soon there were many of man coming to this land near the bottom of Earth.

Sometimes they would fight with the man with the dark skin. The man, with the lighter skin who had just arrived, also took many of her precious animals for his food but soon Mother Nature instructed him how to grow crops and graze others of her animals on the land near the bottom of Earth. On his boats he also brought with him some of the animals that he had been herding on the other lands of Earth with him too.

Mother Nature continues to watch over all of man who live on the land near the bottom of Earth.

She is teaching them how to look after and care for her land near the bottom of Earth, which is so precious to her.

She even lets them dig big holes in the ground and send some bits of the land near the bottom of the Earth to other lands of Earth. This land of hers near the bottom of Earth is just so special that others of man, from other lands of Earth, want some for themselves too.

She even let them make up another name for this special land of hers near the bottom of Earth. Do you know what this new name is?

Australia.

WHO SHIFTED THE RAINBOW?

"The rainbow has been shifted", exclaimed One to Another.

"Well, I don't know who would have done that," replied Another, "It was there yesterday when I looked up into the sky."

Today is sunny and there are just a few clouds to be seen close to the western horizon. It was just yesterday when there were a few light showers of rain and Sun was trying to look at Earth between the clouds, which Weather had placed there, trying to encourage some more rain to fall on this dry land.

"Well," said One, "When I looked out yesterday the rainbow was in the sky and both of its ends were touching the ground."

"Did you try to touch the end that was close to the ground?" asked Another.

"No!" replied One, "I was busy and was not able to spend the time to run over there and touch the end of the rainbow."

"Well perhaps someone else has taken hold of the rainbow and moved it to another place," suggested Another.

"But who would want to shift the rainbow! It should always be there, up in the sky!" Exclaimed One.

One and Another really did not know much about a rainbow except how pretty it is when they see it.

"Perhaps if you did take the time to run over there and take a hold of the rainbow where it touched the ground, then maybe it would still be there for us to look at." Said Another.

"Well, I don't know why you have me doing all of the work!" protested One, "why didn't <u>you</u> go over and take hold of the rainbow where it was touching the ground?"

"Well, if I had known that someone else was going to shift the rainbow, then perhaps I would have gone over there and taken hold of it myself, so that someone else would not take it away." Replied Another.

"Yes perhaps you should have done that, then we would still be able to see the rainbow." Said One.

By the time they had tired themselves out with the argument it was approaching the end of the day. As usual at about this same time every day Sunset was about to show itself.

Weather had positioned some clouds near the west so that when Sun dipped to the horizon some of its last rays of light would show on the clouds. Today the rays of Sun bounced off the clouds and One and Another could see the marvellous display that Sunset was putting on. Sun by now looked like an orange-coloured ball hovering just above the horizon. The bottom of the clouds had a grey tinge to them while the tops of them were a pink colour. As the display of Sunset progressed, this pink colour slowly turned into red and then purple as Sun dipped himself below the horizon.

Several days past and One and Another were still arguing about taking hold of the rainbow so that they could still see it. They eventually came to an agreement.

"I think", said One to Another, "that when we see the rainbow next time, we should both run over and take hold of it where it touches the ground. Then we would be able to see the rainbow all of the time"

Both One and Another agreed that this is what they would do next time they could see the rainbow up in the sky with both of its ends touching the ground.

A week had past and Weather had got some more clouds together which had some water in them. She was going to let most of this water fall from the clouds as rain. The dry ground would soak up the rain very quickly as it was very dry.

Soon the clouds had built up to the south and before too long some light rain began to fall from the clouds to Earth.

One and Another were standing near the top of a hill and could see the rain as it fell from the clouds which Weather had put up there full of water. As the rain fell from the clouds to Earth, the light from Sun would hit the raindrops and the colours of the rainbow were there for everyone to see. It was one of the best rainbows that One or Another had ever seen.

On the underside of the rainbow the colour was purple. The colour next to purple was blue. The colours all blended together as if someone had blended them with a brush. From purple to blue to green then yellow then orange and red at the top of the rainbow. The colours mixed with each other so in between the main colours there was a mixture of these colours.

It was so pretty to see.

The rainbow started from the ground over on their left and arched way up into the sky then bowed down again to touch the ground on their right-hand side.

It was a big rainbow.

As the two of them watched the rainbow, they were both so taken with the sight of it that they completely forgot about their agreement of a few weeks ago. They could see where it touched the ground at both ends and where it raised up in the middle. It was a real bow in its shape and they both watched it with their mouths open in amazement.

Presently the clouds moved over the sky and began to shut out the light from Sun and the rainbow disappeared.

Well, that was just too much for One and Another. They had enjoyed looking at the rainbow so much that they were fixed to the spot and it was a few minutes before they realised that the rainbow had gone.

"Who shifted the rainbow?" asked One of Another.

"Well, you were standing here right next to me, One. Did you see anyone shift the rainbow?" answered Another.

"Well, no! Now that you mention it, no I didn't see who shifted the rainbow."

THE DAY HIGH TIDE WAS LATE.

The plan, which was put together by Mother Nature, Sun, Moon, Day-time, Night-time and Weather is still working to this day. While there have been a few adjustments that have been made over the time that the plan has been working for the place called Earth, most things that happen are working very well.

Sun shines his light and heat in Daytime so the plants can grow and all inhabitants on Earth can see. Following Daytime is Sunset then Night-time so most inhabitants can rest and then Sunrise follows Night-time which in turn is followed again by the next Day-time.

Mostly when Night-time is present, Moon shows herself. Now sometimes this is as a New Moon, First Quarter, Last Quarter or Full Moon. But she is usually present in the night sky.

The other thing which is phenomenal about Moon is that she has this incredible effect on the tides in the oceans of earth as she goes around Earth and through her phases.

There are times when Moon is closer to Earth and at this time the oceans of Earth that are close to her will rise up and be called High tide. When Moon is nearer to the other side of the globe of Earth, the local waters go down or recede and become known as Low tide.

So as the Moon circles Earth each 28 days, she has this incredible effect on the oceans of Earth. The oceans of Earth are in constant movement as Moon travels overhead. There are also currents in the oceans of Earth but we'll talk about those at a later time.

Each day the tide will rise up as Moon gets closer and drops down as Moon gets farther away. On most days there are two times when the tide is rising or full and two times when it falls or is low. So now we know that there is High-tide and Low-tide twice each day.

Because this plan has been going so well for so long everyone has become used to it and has arranged their daily activities around High-tide and Low-tide. As the tide is becoming lower sometimes fish are left stranded on the exposed banks. Some birds, land animals and Man have learned of this and use Low-tide as one of their methods of catching their food. When High-tide is here these low areas are covered with water of the oceans and some fish might swim just to be caught again.

Also, there are some rocks which expose themselves when Low-tide is about, so those oysters and other shellfish which stick on the rocks can be taken by man, animals or birds of Earth. When High-tide is around these are covered in water again. These shellfish survive well on this cycling of Low-tide and High-tide.

Many of the rivers and creeks of earth that drain into the oceans of Earth are affected when either High-tide or Low-tide are present. These rivers and creeks support a lot of Mother Nature's beings and are very dependent on Low-tide and High-tide too.

At the shoreline there usually are some trees call mangroves. When High-tide is here these mangroves help to filter the water to keep it pure. When Low-tide is here the lower parts of them are exposed and need to be covered with seawater just as soon as High-tide can come back.

So, we can see from these details that the presence of either High-tide or Low-tide are very important to life near the edge of the lands of Earth close to the oceans of Earth.

But one day things went astray.

High-tide had been followed by Low-tide for so long that everyone had become used to it, so when High-tide was late, it threw everything into chaos.

On this particular day, everyone was expecting High-tide to be present just as Sunrise was showing itself.

But it just didn't happen.

The low banks were exposed. The rocks were exposed. The tidal creeks were empty. The mangroves were all exposed.

Soon, when Sun began showing himself and applied some heat as well, these places would begin to dry out.

All of the fish that were left stranded on the low banks of mud and sand had been collected and those who collected them were waiting for High tide to bring them some more.

The shellfish which were attached to the rocks are beginning to dry out as they should be under the waters that High tide would bring them. They would need High tide to be here soon or they would dry right out and maybe even die.

The creeks and rivers that should be full now, are empty. All of the animals and other creatures which live there are being stressed too, as they rely so much on the presence of High tide.

The mangroves which rely on the rising and falling tides to do their thing for the sea, can't do their job because the water is just not rising.

If High tide doesn't arrive soon, things would be disastrous. All of the beings which rely so much on High tide would really be left high and dry.

All of the beings which are so badly affected by the lack of High tide called on Mother Nature to intercept before things get too bad.

If High-tide is not here, then how can Low-tide follow? What is going to happen if Low-tide is followed by another Low-tide? What will happen to all of those beings that are so reliant on High tide being here?

These are the questions that were put to Mother Nature and she spent a little time to get some answers.

So that everything did not dry out too much, Mother Nature called on Weather to blow up a storm over the ocean to create some rain that would fall onto the dry, parched parts of the coastline, that were so badly affected by High-tide not being here. This rain did in fact stop them from drying out too much but it was not seawater, it was fresh water. While this fresh water would be good to stop things from drying out too much, all of the creatures really did need the seawater that High tide provided for them.

While this rain was falling, Mother Nature was searching for High tide.

She knew that Moon was in the right place, so there was no problem there. She knew that Sun did not have much effect on High-tide or Low-tide, so that was no problem there. She knew that although Weather does have some effect on High-tide and Low-tide that today that was not the case because Weather had just changed from mild and sunny to wet and windy.

She just could not find out where High tide was.

It was becoming so late now that very soon Low tide would be here again.

But none of Mother Nature's creatures knew what would happen if Low-tide was followed by Low-tide.

Well, that is what was about to happen. High-tide just would not be here today so they will just have to be happy with seeing Low-tide twice today.

So, it was a very long day for everyone who was expecting to see High-tide between the two Low-tides. So Low tide arrived and stayed for the normal amount of time that she would normally stay. After Low-tide had been here for the second time today, things are about to alter.

Presently the waters began to rise. It was so slow that almost no-one saw it rising.

Mother Nature was so busy trying to find High tide that she didn't have time to notice that the level of the water was slowly becoming higher. Weather was so busy with her change of weather and trying to put the right amount of rain on those that needed it, didn't notice the water rising.

But Moon had got herself into the right position and she could see High tide as he was coming in. She didn't know where he was when he was supposed to be here last time. It was a mystery to her. She just didn't know!

As High-tide got closer, there were lots of bubbles rising in the water as High-tide brought in the water from the ocean and made the level of the water near the coast of the land of Earth higher.

Soon the rising of the water was allowing the mangroves to do their job.

Soon all of the sand and mud banks were covered in water.

Soon all of the rocks were covered in water.

Soon all of the creeks and rivers were full of water.

Shortly things returned to normal as those who depended on High-tide replenished themselves in the seawater that was provided for them by High-tide.

The shellfish which attach themselves to the rocks are happy now that they are under the salty seawater that they depend on.

The creatures that live in and around the tidal creeks and rivers are happy too as they are also getting their share of the seawater that is provided for them when High-tide is here.

Man, animals and birds who collect the fish which are left behind when High-tide goes away are happy, because now they might find some more of the fish left behind for them to collect.

The mangroves at the edge of the sea were happy, because now they could be successful in their job of helping to keep the oceans pure.

It wasn't too long before everything returned to normal at the coastline of the land of Earth where the oceans of Earth meet and where Mother Nature's creatures depend on High-tide to follow Low-tide.

No-one ever did find out why High-tide was late but they are all happy that he is back and still follows Low-tide.

Everything has returned to normal now and this made everyone happy, as they can again do what they have to do without worrying about where High tide was, the day he was late.

THE TIME WHEN SUN WAS CROOK

Sun really does play such an important part in the plan which they have all put together.

He provides the light and heat when Night-time is not here.

This light and heat allows for all of Mother Nature's plants to live happily and this light and heat also allows for Mother Nature's animals and man to live happily on the place called Earth.

In fact, when Sun provides his light and heat everyone is happy.

How he does this is not fully understood but he has some gas inside him that when it rises to the surface, ignites and burns very hotly. So hot that nothing can get close to him or they will just burn up and disappear. Sometimes there are little spots where extra gas is ignited and these little spots burn a lot hotter. This causes a lot of other things to happen as the result of these "hot spots".

But he just keeps on burning his gas and providing Mother Nature with all the light and heat that she requires for her Earth.

But a long, long time ago, well before Mother Nature put man onto earth, Sun got crook.

Sun was not sure what the problem was. Perhaps his gas was not rising to the surface fast enough to keep his fires burning.

Perhaps the fires did not burn hot enough for another reason, he just didn't know.

He wasn't feeling too good but he just could not figure out just what the problem was. It didn't affect him too much. There was no discomfort. He wasn't really sick, just a bit crook.

With Sun being "Just a bit crook" had some very disturbing consequences for earth and Mother Nature.

You see the light and heat which Sun used to provide for Mother Nature's plan to work so well had diminished. There was in fact less light and heat arriving at the surface of Earth.

Well, you say, what difference would a little less light and heat make to Earth? It can't be much. Well think again.

By this time in the development of Earth, Mother Nature has positioned two ice caps. There was one at the top of Earth and there was one at the bottom of Earth. Now while there was just the right amount of light and heat arriving to hit the surface of Earth it kept the ice caps in their place. Mother Nature used this as a tool to help her to maintain the balance of ice on her Earth.

Of course, with their being less light and heat then the ice caps could escape and spread further out on Earth.

This is like leaving the gate open and the cows get out and begin to wander, isn't it?

The light and heat that was arriving from Sun was the only way that Mother Nature had of controlling the amount of ice that she wanted to keep on Earth.

So now that the ice caps had escaped they began spreading out towards the equator, which is supposed to be the hottest place on Earth.

Slowly but surely, they crept forward, spreading out over the oceans of Earth and slowly but surely spreading out over some of the lands of Earth as well.

The ice caps did move forward very slowly, so for the most part, only some of the trees and shrubs which Mother Nature had planted on Earth had time to adapt to the ice caps moving over them. But there are also many which did not adapt to this new cold that they had never seen before and they just died off and disappeared from the surface of earth.

The animals which Mother Nature had put on earth could move about quite freely but there were still some of them who were very slow and could not move out of the way of the escaping ice caps. Also, some of these were land animals and they reached edge of the lands of Earth and could not go any further. Their options were to swim on the oceans of Earth to another piece of the lands of Earth or drown in the process. Another option was to remain and try to adapt or to die from the freezing cold of the ice as it approached.

It was a very difficult time for everyone except the ice caps. The ice caps were very happy to be spreading out all over Earth after having been cooped up in their tiny little area just at the top and the bottom of Earth. They were having a ball. They were doing what they did best, making things cold.

It was not long before the ice caps which used to cover only about fifteen percent of the surface of Earth had escaped out over an area of fifty percent of the surface of Earth.

Poor old Mother Nature's Earth had become very cold.

Because Sun still hadn't recovered from being crook, he still could not send enough light and heat to earth to stop the escaping ice caps as they spread out over the surface of Earth.

So, because Sun was still crook, the ice caps continued to be cold all over the area that they had covered. There was still enough light and heat arriving at the surface of Earth to stop the ice caps from escaping enough to cover all of Earth, so Mother Nature was at least happy with that.

It was many millennia that Sun remained crook and for the same amount of time the ice caps continued to keep things so very cold over the parts of Earth that they had covered.

The lands of Earth that are covered by the ice caps are now so cold that nothing will grow on them. The oceans of Earth that are covered by the ice caps are so cold that not very much can live in them.

Mother Nature was very upset at this because she has spent so much of her time and effort into putting all of the animals and plants on Earth to make it her special place.

She was very disappointed.

But she pressed on and helped those animals and plants that she could, to find better places but she had simply run out of places. Every place was full. She couldn't fit any more into the places that were not covered by the escaping ice caps.

Presently Sun would begin to feel a little better and some of his fires would burn a little hotter for a while but he would just drop back to being crook again. But Mother Nature did notice that while Sun was burning a little hotter, the ice caps did move back just a little. She would need to help Sun to get better so that they could work together to resolve this problem of the escaping ice caps.

It took many more millennia before they could work out the cause of the problem with Sun's health.

One day, he noticed that he was feeling better for longer periods of time. And each time he felt better his fires burned hotter and the ice caps receded just a little.

Slowly but slowly, Sun got better and slowly but slowly he go hotter and slowly but slowly the ice caps began to recede.

Soon Mother Nature helped Sun to get back to his old self and he soon had his fires burning fiercely again.

Now it was not long before Sun was back to his old self. His gas was rising to the surface just as it was before. His fires were burning just as hot as they were before. Just the right amount of heat and light was arriving at the surface of Earth again.

Now Mother Nature could see that the ice caps had begun retreating.

It did take a long time but slowly, ever so slowly the ice caps retreated.

Sun kept on shining down and sending his heat and light while Mother Nature worked with the plants and animals, so that they could return to their old places.

After a long time, Mother Nature and Sun had got the ice caps under control again and had them back to their rightful place.

Once again there was an ice cap at the top of Earth and another at the bottom of Earth, just where Mother Nature wanted them to be.

This was the balance that she wanted. It had worked so well before and that is how she wanted it to stay for ever more.

After the ice caps had been under control again and kept in the correct place, Mother Nature had time to reflect on what had happened.

She could now see that seeds from some of her plants had germinated and had begun to grow again.

Some of the animals which had been displaced when the ice caps escape had now returned to their rightful place and they were happy.

Mother Nature stood back and took a good look at her Earth and could see where the ice had retreated from but that area was now recovering from its period of extreme cold.

She could see that her earth was returning to normal and she was happy.

This escaping of the ice caps and their spreading over so much of her Earth, Mother Nature called the Ice Age.

WHO PUT THE STARS IN THE SKY?

One and Another had just finished a day of hunting and were on their way back to the cave to bring some food for their mates to cook for the family.

They had left the cave a bit late because it was wet this morning and the fire in the cave had kept it warm and comfortable.

The rain which fell during the night had passed over by the time Sunrise had finished his display and the day had been warm and sunny. The air was very clear now that the rain had washed away the dust of the last few dry weeks.

Because of the late start to their hunting trip, they would be very late in returning to the cave where their families are waiting for them.

Sunset had just finished his display and they still had several hours to go before they would be back at the cave.

"There is not much food around now, so soon we'll need to find another cave that is closer to where we hunt," said One to Another.

"Yes that would be much better and then we could stay in bed longer and still hunt our food and be back before dark" replied Another.

They trudged on, keeping to the path that had become well worn.

As Night-time began to gain its darkness, they had difficulty in seeing the path and several times they bumped into trees and boulders.

"I think we should stop here for the night," said One to Another, "and we can continue on in the morning".

"But the family will go hungry tonight if we don't get this food back to them before too long," replied Another.

"They are old enough by now that a late meal won't hurt them", said One, "besides we won't get anything to eat either if we don't get back to the cave tonight".

"Perhaps we need to find a warm place to sleep for the night," suggested Another.

They were on a low hill where there were a few boulders and some low scrub so they arranged some of the scrub to form a mattress for their bed. Soon they had a comfortable place to lie down and the rocks gave them some warmth.

One of the reasons that it was so dark was that Moon was in its "new moon phase" and was on the other side of Earth. All One and Another knew was that Moon was not in the sky. It was many years before they would learn why Moon could not be seen some nights.

Although Moon was not present in the Night-time's sky, the stars were brilliantly visible in Night-time's sky.

Because they were out in the open for the first time for a very long time they could see the stars in the sky. In the cave the stars are hidden from them by the roof of the cave.

One and Another laid back in the bush bed and looked straight up into the sky and could see the stars that were overhead. When they looked to right they could see more stars. When they looked to the left they could see even more stars. In fact, everywhere that they looked they could see a lot more stars. There were so many more stars in Night-time's sky than they knew numbers for, so they were not able to count how many there was.

There were some very bright stars. There were some stars that looked like they were blinking. There were stars that looked like they were changing colour. There was a string of some very tiny stars that even looked like star dust up there in the sky.

"Can you touch that big star?" Asked One of Another.

Another stretched his arm as long as he could but he could not touch that big star. He got out of bed and climbed up to the top of the rocks that was near them and reached up but still he could not touch that big star. He took hold of his spear and prodded towards the big star that was above them but still he could not touch the star.

"No", replied Another, "the star looks so close but I just cannot touch it".

"Well then it must be a lot further away than it looks," commented One.

Another lay down again and they just looked at the stars.

While they were looking at the stars they thought that they could see some shapes that the stars made if you drew an imaginary line between them.

One of these shapes were a spear. This occurred when they could see three stars in a line.

Another group of stars looked like a cross that was on its side. To find this group of stars, both One and Another were looking to the south. There were two other stars close by that were also very bright.

While they looked at the stars they looked slowly from right to left and from in front of them and to behind them. They were so enthralled with the spectacular sight of the stars that it took a long time for them to look at them all.

By the time they got back to look at those on the right again, some were out of sight behind the rocks. Another got up from the bed and looked over the top of the rocks and then he could see those stars which were missing.

The stars had shifted.

But One and Another had been busy all day and had walked a long way, so presently they drifted off to sleep. They slept very soundly.

Well before Night-time began to lose its darkness, One woke up Another and they could still see the stars in the sky but they were all in a different place. Those groups of stars which looked like a cross were now upside down to what they were before. Some of the other shapes which they could imagine last night could not be seen.

Soon, as Night-time began to lose its darkness, the stars began to fade. Presently Sunrise would show himself and One and Another started walking. Then Daytime showed himself and One and Another continued on their way back to their caves and their families. The food which they carried was still a load on their backs.

As they walked along they began talking about their experience with seeing all of those stars in Night-time's sky.

"Those stars made a real picture in Night-time's sky didn't they?" said One to Another.

"Yes, they look so close but are so far away that I can't reach them but they are very bright and pretty to see", replied Another after a short while. He had been thinking and presently he had a question of One.

"Who put the stars in the sky?"

"I don't know who put the stars in the sky", answered One who had been thinking along similar lines. "Perhaps we should ask someone else and find out if they know who put the stars in the sky."

They continued on their walk towards their cave and they asked everyone and everything that they passed the same question, "who put the stars in the sky?"

Everyone and everything that they asked gave the same answer to the question, "I don't know but I'm sure someone will", was the reply.

Soon all of man, on the lands of Earth, were asking the same question as they had all become interested to find out the answer of "who put the stars in the sky".

It seems that it was not only one and another who wanted to know the answer but everyone did. Man, animal, plants.

With the question being asked around of everyone, soon Mother Nature heard everyone asking this same question so she gathered them all to her and told them of how the stars got put in the sky.

She told everyone about what happened so long, long ago when there was this big, big bang and at that time everything exploded and sent stuff everywhere.

Right through space it all went.

Some stuff joined up and become Earth. Other stuff joined up and become Moon. Some other stuff joined up and become Sun. Other stuff joined up and become the stars and went a long, long way away from Earth so they would not hurt Earth.

Some of these stars were big and some of these stars were a lot smaller and some were so tiny that they all got together and formed a cloud which can still be seen up there in Night-time's sky and is called the Milky Way. Some of the stars are able to have their own light, just like our Sun while others are there just to reflect the light from Sun back to us so that we can enjoy looking at the sky at Night-time.

"So there", said Mother Nature, "You have the answer to the question of who put the stars in the sky".

Mother Nature, after giving this information to everyone, went back to what she always does best and that is looking after her Earth.

SEASONS

When Mother Nature was putting together her plan for her place called Earth, she was having difficulty with the adjusting of the temperature of the different places where her plants were growing and her animals were living.

She wasn't too sure about how to fix the problem.

Sometimes things were getting too hot or too wet or too cold or too dry. After many years of studying the problem and watching her plants and animals struggling to cope with these extremes every day, she just could not seem to find a solution to the problem, so she slept on the problem as this had helped her so many times previously. When she awoke from her sleep it came to her! "I know! I'll get Seasons to help so that there will be some time for rain and some time for sun. That should help the plants to grow at just about the right rate so they won't take over everything. It might even help the animals to fit in better."

Before she started making her plans with her old friend, Seasons, she took some time to sit back and look carefully at what was happening with the place she called Earth. She knew it was going to be a big job and she wanted to get this one right the first time so she did a lot of studying of the problem.

She had sorted out the problem of how far her Earth should be from Sun. She has got Moon sorted out into her path of rotating around Earth, so the next thing she did, was to cause Earth to tilt or wobble just a little bit.

She reckoned that if Earth should tilt in its rotation each year, she could have Sun shining on one part of it, while the other part cooled and then for the next part of the year, Sun could shine on the other part of Earth and allow it to warm up just a bit. She reckoned that with this gentle warming she should be able to control the amount of warmth that Sun could put onto Earth and not allow one section of it to become too cold or too warm.

After a lot of thought of how to do this job, Mother Nature made some marks on Earth. Right around the middle of Earth, at its widest part she put in a mark and called this mark the Equator. South of the Equator she put another mark. This she called The Tropic of Capricorn, after an old friend of hers. Next she put another mark above the Equator and she called this one the Tropic of Cancer after another old friend. Both of these marks are the same distance from the Equator and Mother Nature reckoned that if she put them about twenty-three and a half degrees from the Equator, it should work out just right

Now she had to make Earth wobble just enough so that for half of the year, Sun could shine directly down on Earth between the Equator and the Tropic of Cancer and for the other half of the year, Earth would wobble just a bit allowing Sun to shine between the Equator and the Tropic of Capricorn.

Now, she didn't want Earth to shift too quickly as this might upset some of the fine balance which she already had put into her project, so she made Earth move slowly and it would take a quarter of a year for Earth to move so that Sun would shine on the area between the Equator and the Tropic of Cancer. For the next quarter of the year Earth would move back to its original position. Now to make things complete she needed Earth to wobble so that Sun would shine on the area between the Equator and the Tropic of Capricorn. So, for the next quarter of the year Earth would wobble just a bit so that Sun would shine directly above the area between the Equator and the Tropic of Capricorn and then for the next quarter of the year it would return to its position directly above the Equator.

After many, many years she was able to train Earth so that it would do as she wanted and to her way of thinking this should fix that problem of overheating or overcooling for the most of earth.

After Mother Nature was satisfied that she had Earth wobbling between the Tropic of Cancer and the tropic of Capricorn she decided that she could create some seasons that would work in with this wobbling of Earth.

The area above the Equator she would call the Northern Hemisphere while the area below the Equator she would call the Southern Hemisphere. Now she could separate the two sections so that she could set up some seasons for them.

Now, Mother Nature's friend, Seasons had four daughters. Their names are Summer, Autumn, Winter and Spring.

Mother Nature and Seasons worked out a plan and they knew that they needed four periods of the year and these four periods just seemed to suit the personalities of the four daughters.

Summer was a bit hot headed and had red hair, so they named the hottest season after her, Summer.

Spring had a very light step with a bubbly personality, so the period of light and growth could be named after her, Spring.

The daughter whose name was Winter was always dark and stormy, so they could name the darker period of the year after her, Winter.

So that left Autumn. She just didn't seem to fit anywhere in particular so they thought that they would name the remaining period after her, Autumn.

Mother Nature and Seasons worked tirelessly for a long time to make sure that they had covered all of the points that were so important that needed to be covered and dealt with.

Just to make sure that this is correct, Mother Nature made sure that Sun would be directly above the Tropic of Cancer in the northern hemisphere's summer and directly above the Tropic of Capricorn in the southern hemisphere's summer.

As it takes Earth half a year to move to allow Sun to shine above the Equator up to the Tropic of Cancer and back again, this time would be split into three parts.

The first part would be the second half of spring. This is followed by Summer as Sun is shining right over the Tropic of Cancer. Summer is followed by Autumn. As Earth moves so that Sun shines over Southern Hemisphere, Autumn of the Northern Hemisphere is completed and Spring begins for the Southern Hemisphere.

While Sun is shining over the Northern Hemisphere it is Spring and at the same time it is Autumn in the Southern Hemisphere.

So, while it is warmer in the northern hemisphere it is cooler in the southern hemisphere and when it is cool in the northern hemisphere it is warmer in the southern hemisphere. When it is Winter in the northern hemisphere it is also Summer in the southern hemisphere.

So, Mother Nature gets to know the periods of the year that they have named after the daughters of her friend, Seasons:

Winter, when it is cooler and it usually rains.

Spring, when it begins to warm and many plants grow very well and have their flowers.

Summer, when it is hotter and only rains near the Equator.

Autumn, when many plants and animals prepare for the next season of winter.

The situation of having Summer in the northern hemisphere while it was Winter in the southern hemisphere took a long time for everyone to get used to. It was so confusing to have summer in one place while it was winter in another. The old system was just so good.

But Mother Nature would have none of this argument. She was adamant that this new system of hers with the introduction of the different seasons in each hemisphere was going to work, so she did work hard and finally convinced everyone that it would be for the best.

Many, many years passed and everyone soon got used to Mother Nature's new system. It was such a good system, in fact, it's such a good system that it is still working today.

These new friends of Mother Nature's have been doing their job for many, many years and now the plants and animals on Mother Nature's Earth have adjusted to the seasons and they are all able to prosper, just as Mother nature wanted.

The only thing that Mother Nature was worried about was that she could not seem to control the rain that fell in the tropics. It just seemed to fall all the time. But this problem sorted itself out as some different types of plants and animals soon got used to this constant rain. Those of them that didn't get used to the weather shifted away from the tropics and found an area that suited them better.

So once again Mother Nature has done such a great job of fixing the problem and soon everybody, including her, is satisfied.

Earth now works so well, as everything flourishes with Mother Nature's Seasons and she is happy.

WEATHER

Whilst you've been reading these stories you will have noticed that Mother Nature relied so heavily on Weather to help her sort out some of the things that needed to be sorted out in this project that she had started so many, many years ago.

Sometimes when Mother Nature had a problem she would ask Weather to step in and help her to sort out and solve these problems.

That time, so long ago when Mother Nature and Weather attempted to fix the problem with the desert, they did work together so well but unfortunately that problem could not be rectified.

Weather also helps Mother Nature with Sunset and Sunrise by sometimes sending in some clouds so that everyone can appreciate a spectacular Sunrise or a colourful Sunset.

Whether also works very well with the four daughters of Seasons. She knows when it is the correct time to send in the clouds and make it rain, because that usually is the Winter Season. She also knows which season does not need the clouds to be in the sky, this would usually be the Season of Summer. When it is Spring and Autumn, she knows just how much cloud to provide, so that just the right amount of rain should fall in the right place at the right time. She knows also just when to move the clouds so that the correct amount of sunshine falls onto the surface of Earth.

That time so long ago, when Mother Nature got angry and her trembling caused the volcanos to spew all of that hot gas and lava into the air, it was Weather who got the wind to blow and spread the dust and gas all over the face of Earth so it wouldn't cause too much trouble. She also made it rain on the dust so that it would be sent back to the surface of Earth and not make the air dirty for too long.

Weather also causes the winds and breezes to blow, so that those of Man from the lands of Earth could use their ships to travel on the oceans of Earth. This wind and breeze also helps many of the plants with the pollinating of their flowers

Near the Equator, Weather causes those circular winds that make it rain in the tropics. In the southern hemisphere these are known as Cyclones and travel in a clockwise direction. These circular winds are called Hurricanes in the northern hemisphere and rotate in an anticlockwise direction.

So, you can see that Weather has a big job to do, just to help Mother Nature with her project.

So, over the many, many years which Mother Nature has been involved in this project called Earth, Weather has been a great assistance and has helped Mother Nature in so many ways since she has been involved with Mother Nature's pet project.

Mother Nature now doesn't need to call on Weather to do those regular things anymore, because Weather knows just what to do and gets the jobs done without Mother Nature having to get involved with any of it, unless she has a special job for Weather to do for her.

Over the years that Weather, with the assistance of Seasons and her four daughters, has been helping Mother Nature, She has developed some special activities that have helped make Earth such a special place. Weather makes the breezes and winds blow over the oceans of earth and when this happens, it collects some of the water which has evaporated from the surface of the oceans of Earth. This evaporated water rises up into the air as very tiny droplets of water and forms into clouds. As more and more of these tiny droplets collect, the clouds get bigger and bigger. As these clouds get bigger and bigger they are shifted along with the winds and breezes. When Mother Nature finds the right place, she will make the tiny droplets fall as rain. Usually she makes this rain fall over the lands of Earth. But sometimes this rain also falls over the oceans of Earth.

There are many places where Weather can make this rain fall. Sometimes it will fall as light rain but sometimes it might fall as heavy rain. There are times when the heavy rain might cause flooding and this could cause some problems particularly on flat country.

When this rain reaches the ground it turns back into water again.

This water is used by the plants that Mother Nature has put onto Earth so that they can survive. The animals also drink this water so they too can survive. Man uses this water to drink and wash in and after many years has learnt how to use this water to grow crops.

So, you see this rain is very important to the lives of all the beings on Earth.

It is just so important!

There are some places on Earth that might be closer to the top of Earth and some places that are closer to the bottom of Earth where it gets very cold in their Winter seasons. Sometimes during the season of Winter, Weather will make the clouds behave a little bit differently and make snow which falls to the ground. This snow lays on the ground and forms a soft fluffy white carpet. Sometimes this fluffy white carpet is very thin if there is just a small amount of snow and sometimes when there is a lot of snow, that carpet can become very thick.

If Weather makes the Winter season very, very cold, in these places closer to the top of Earth and closer to the bottom of Earth, the snow can turn into ice. Sometimes this ice may be very thin but sometimes this ice can become very thick if there is a lot of snow or even if rain falls onto it. This ice can cover the ground and even cover the lakes and rivers and sometimes even parts of the oceans of Earth.

Many of the animals and some of Man have learnt to use the ice for different things. Man can have fun and skate on the ice but it is very cold. Some of Man who live in the very, very cold places of Earth even make their homes out of blocks of ice.

These seasons of Winter which can be very cold in those places which are close to the top of earth and close to the bottom of earth are followed by spring. The season of Spring is when the sun begins to shine more warmly again and this sunshine melts the ice and snow. The water which comes from the melting of ice and snow finds its way into Creeks and Rivers. When this water finds its way back into the Creeks and Rivers it can sometimes fill them and sometimes flow over the banks. When this water flows over the banks it is referred to as flooding. Just how much flooding there is depends upon how much water is in the creek or river. If there is not much water in the creek or river then they may not be much flooding but if there is a lot of water in the creek or river then the flooding may cover a lot of country. This is one of the ways that Mother Nature's uses to replenish the land and supply water for the plants and animals, who live far away from the Creeks and Rivers.

As the sun begins to warm up the land in the season of spring, the small annual plants begin to grow and by the end of spring they will have reached their full size. This season of spring is also the time when most of Mother Nature's plants grow abundantly and bear their flowers.

This growth provides a lot of food for the animals that need the food during the long and sometimes hot summer.

Even in the parts of Earth that are away from the top or the bottom of Earth and enjoy very comfortable weather, have the same things happen as the seasons change.

But things don't always go the way that either Mother Nature or Weather or Seasons and her daughters plan or want.

Sometimes Weather just cannot get the clouds to stop letting the rain fall from the clouds to the ground.

Now, this happens frequently near the tropics and everything in that area of Earth had learnt to accept this excess rain which turns into water and have learnt to cope with the problem.

But when this happens in a place where it was not expected and the plants and animals and the surface of Earth are not prepared for it, many problems can occur.

In the Land near the Bottom of Earth, most of the rainfall is near the edge of the land close to the edge of the Oceans of Earth. This is where most of Man have assembled and the growth of the plants suits the activities of Man and his animals. Here, they have learnt to accept and live with this heavier rainfall. But further from the edge of the land the rainfall normally diminishes until, close to the centre of the Land near the Bottom of Earth, the rain only falls once every few years and even then it is just a small amount. This small amount of rain is just enough to sustain the growth of the plants that support the animals that Mother Nature has put there. This keeps everything in the fine balance that Mother Nature wants for her place call Earth.

But sometimes it just goes wrong!

Sometimes it doesn't even rain for long periods of time.

The Land near the bottom of Earth suffers badly when these situations happen.

Because the land near the bottom of Earth is so diverse, there are many factors which tell the four daughters of Seasons to do stuff, like make it rain or make it not rain. They usually work well with Weather but when communications break down between them, these problems seem to happen.

If Weather doesn't send in the rain when it is the Winter Season, the land stays dry. The longer that it doesn't rain, the longer the land stays dry. Sometimes Weather makes a mistake and it doesn't rain for several years.

Now, this does cause some very real problems for so many of Mother Nature's plants and animals. They all do need to have the Seasons work for them and when this problem occurs it just upsets their systems.

They don't get to drink very much.

Because there is no rain to cool things down, they can get very hot.

When the ground is so dry and the wind blows, a lot of dust is created. So, when it is dry for a long time, Weather needs to be very careful not to make the wind blow too much or else a lot of the land would be blown away as dust. This dust even creates more problems for everything that lives near the middle of the land near the bottom of Earth. It is not very nice living in a very dusty place. The dust blocks up the pores of the plants and they suffer. The dust can damage the eyes of the animals and also those of Man who live near there.

These long dry spells in the weather are called droughts. Sometimes these may last for as little as a few weeks to many years. Sometimes even as many as twenty years without rain.

That's very dry.

Many plants can die because of this drought.

Many animals can die from this drought.

Man, too can become very ill if this drought lasts for too long.

But the drought always seems to come to an end.

Sometimes this end can be gradual or it can be sudden.

When it is gradual that is good because everything can then adapt easily to the new weather. When it is not gradual sometimes it can be disastrous.

At the end of a drought, Weather makes it rain gently for a while. If the change is gradual sometimes this rain will stop after a short time then begin again.

But sometimes Weather forgets to stop the rains and instead of falling mainly near the edge of the Land as it usually does, it continues to fall in great amounts a long way away from the edge of the land.

Now mostly this land is very flat with a very gentle slope to the centre of the land.

When this unusual rainfall event happens, it dumps very large amounts of rainwater onto the land away from the edges of the Land of Earth. Sometimes this rainfall lasts for just a day or two and everything receives just enough rainfall or maybe just a little bit more than is needed.

But when the rainfall continues and more big heavy clouds get blown over the centre of the Land, more and more rain continues to fall.

At the beginning of this excessive rainfall, the ground gets covered in water. As the rain continues the water spreads out and continues to get deeper. This water which has fallen from the sky as rain spreads out over the land and finds all of the low areas and flows in that direction.

The more rain that falls to the ground, the deeper it gets on the ground and eventually there can be a flood here too. A flood is when there is more water on the ground than usual and it gets deeper and deeper as the rain continues to fall.

Soon the water is flowing into the creeks and the creeks accept the water until they have been filled to the banks. Many of these creeks are connected to rivers and soon the water flows from the creeks into the rivers and as the rain continues to fall they all become deeper and deeper. As the rain continues to fall, the water gets deeper over the land and in the creeks and in the rivers. The rivers take as much water as they can and send it on its way downstream into areas where it has not rained. If the rain could stop now, it would be good and not cause too much trouble but if it does continue to fall, it does cause problems.

If the creeks and rivers are not able to hold all of the water within their banks, it must spill over the edge of them and out onto the flat country. This is one way that Mother Nature plans to provide water to that area where it does not rain very much.

As the water becomes deeper and deeper as it spreads out over the land, more and more land becomes flooded. Soon the water has travelled over a large area of the land far away from the creeks and rivers.

All the birds can see when they fly is water.

Water to the front of them!

Water to the left and to the right and water behind them!

In fact, water everywhere!

It is only the trees and some hills and mounds of rocks which they can see above the water.

Those of man who live and hunt in this area, find that they must shift their homes to the highest of the ground, so they have a dry bed to sleep on and a dry place to cook their food. Some of them have their homes flooded or washed away in the flood.

Slowly the water spreads out over the land until much of the land is covered by water.

The downstream rivers fill up as the water from upstream finds its way downstream to them. As they fill, they too allow the water to spread out over the land.

Weather eventually realizes her error and gets the rain to stop falling and sends the clouds away, to let their water fall somewhere else.

After many, many days and soon, many weeks, this water that has spread out over the land finds its way into a large lake near the centre of the land near the Bottom of Earth and flows into it, even if the rains stop. This lake is usually dry but as soon as the water from the flood reaches it, it transforms into a magnificently large lake.

Before long there are fish in the lake and very soon after that, there are many birds to feed on the fish in the lake. There are so many birds on the lake that the sky is full of them as they fly about searching for mates and food.

In this time of flooding of the land near the centre of the Land near the Bottom of Earth, is the best time for many of Mother Nature's birds to reproduce. The abundant food supply keeps them well fed and soon they grow to enormous numbers. As the young birds learn to fly, the waters begin to recede and the birds head back to the coast again.

Usually when this land is flooded, there is plenty of sunshine so the land is warm. This is the best opportunity for all of the plants to grow again. They have the moisture that they need and they have warm soil to grow in, so soon the whole of the land near the centre of the land near the Bottom of Earth is a mass of colour.

Mother Nature and Weather, with the help of the four daughters of Season, stand back and admire their handiwork. It looks so good and they are pleased with their efforts even if it did go wrong and someone had been inconvenienced.

Soon, Weather gets things back to normal and does as Mother Nature wants by keeping things in balance. She gets just the right amount of rain to fall in the right place at the right time again.

Not long after this event everyone is happy once more.

THE TIME STICK

That long night that One and Another had spent under the stars away from their families got them to wonder at the sight of what they had seen in the heavens above their sleeping place that night. They had accepted Mother Nature's explanation of "who put the stars in the sky" and this information had kept them satisfied for a very long time.

Now it seems that both One and Another are able to expand their thoughts and are thinking a bit deeper than they had in the past.

Now they came to wonder how is it, that at some times of the year the nights get shorter and at other times of the year the nights become longer.

This difference of the length of the nights was very difficult to recognise because it changes just a minute or so each day and that small time variation is easy to overlook.

One and Another could tell the time by the sun during the day and they know that in summer, Sunrise happens a lot sooner than Sunrise does during the winter. Over the years they had learnt to look at the shadows to determine the time of day.

In the mornings, the sun would shine on the east side of the Time-stick that they had stuck in the ground for the purpose of telling the time and a long shadow would show on the ground to the west of the Time-stick. When the sun was directly over-head, the shadow of the Time-stick was very short.

The shortest shadow of the Time-stick occurs when it is summertime and Sun is almost directly overhead.

(Now this changes, depending on where you are in the southern hemisphere. Closer to the Tropic of Capricorn the shorter the shadow is, as Sun is directly overhead. Between the Tropic of Capricorn and the Equator the shadow becomes longer again but is north of the Time-stick.)

But One and Another are about 28 degrees south of the Equator and the shadow is short but to the south of the Time-stick at midday.

As the day progresses the shadow of the Time-stick moves around and by the evening, just before Sunset is about to show itself, the shadow is long and pointing towards the east.

One and Another have spent some time studying the shadows of the Time-stick and find out that while the shadow of the Time-stick moves during Daytime, there is no shadow that helps them to tell the time while Nigh-time is here.

When it was not cloudy in the Wintertime, they also took some time to watch the shadows of their Time-stick.

In the winter mornings just as Sunrise had finished his display and Sun was shining down on Earth, they looked at the Time-stick. Sun was shining on the east side of the Time-stick and casting a shadow to the west. But because it is Winter, the sun does not shine directly down but at an angle and the shadow points a bit to the south of west. Likewise at midday the shadow is longer than it was in summer but still points to the south. As the winter's day progresses, the shadow moves around and points to the east and just a little to the south.

One and Another had made some marks upon the ground at the end of the shadow during the day but one day it rained and washed away all their marks.

They had marked the end of the shadow at the longest day and the shortest day but after those marks had become washed away they decided to move their Time-stick to a better place, where their marks would not be washed away.

On the hill not far from their cave they found a flat rock that had a hole in it and into this hole they stuck their Time-stick.

There was enough room around the Time-stick to make marks on the ground so they could record the movement of the shadow as the shadow moved around the Time-stick. They had found a hard stone in the creek and this was hard enough to mark the rock that held their Time-stick.

Now as the days progressed they continued to mark the flat rock around the base of their Time-stick with the marks with the hard stone.

All of these marks were to the south of the Time-stick and the shortest shadows were marked when the weather was the hottest during the summer. During the winter the marks were longer as Sun moved well to the north of where One and Another lived in their cave.

One of the marks they had made was on the shortest day of the year and another was made at the end of the shadow on the longest day.

One and Another knew what the marks are but they did not know what all of these marks mean. So, they pondered these things between themselves for a considerable length of time.

They didn't know anyone else who had spent the time to study the movement of the shadows as they did. In fact, everyone else thought that they were a bit stupid to draw marks on the rock as the shadow moved around the Time-stick.

It seems that One and Another may have been the first scientists on Earth.

Mother Nature had taken notice of what One and Another were doing and she was very impressed, as now Man was beginning to understand her work on Earth.

One day she took the two of them aside and told them the Season of Winter, Spring, Autumn and Summer and how she had arranged them.

She told One and Another she was impressed that they had taken the time to study her work on Earth with their markings of the shadow as it moved around the Time-stick.

She pointed out that the longest day was called "Summer Solstice" and this occurred on the 21st of December.

The she went on to tell them of the shortest day that they had marked on the stone at the base of the Time-stick was the "Winter Solstice" and this occurs on the 20th of June.

"But" said Mother Nature, "there is one more piece of information that you didn't mark on the stone at the base of the Time-stick that is important and that is the "Equinox."

"The Equinox also happens twice each year and this is when the hours of night-time and the hours of daytime are equal. Or if you like the day-light hours are the same number as the night-darkness hours."

"Autumn Equinox occurs on the 20th of March while the Spring Equinox happens on the 22nd of September, each and every year."

Well, One and Another were enthralled with this input from Mother Nature and were so proud that she had taken the time from her busy schedule to tell them all of this important information.

Mother Nature continued with some additional information but perhaps One and Another were not able to absorb this because although they could understand days, minutes did not mean anything to them because clocks had not been invented yet.

"It's 184 days between the winter solstice and the summer solstice so that means that each day is one minute and twelve seconds longer as the days lengthen from ten hours and eighteen minutes long to thirteen hours and fifty-nine minutes long."

Both One and Another stood with their mouths agape at this, as it was clear to Mother Nature that it did not make any sense to them.

When Mother Nature was satisfied that they had as much information as their learning would allow, she left them alone to absorb the details of what she had told them. She went back to do what she had been doing for such a long time now and that was to care for her project of Earth.

One and Another felt so important that now they had some knowledge and so they went about telling everyone else what Mother Nature had told them. One and Another shared all of their experiences with the marking of the shadows of their Time-stick and how Mother Nature had helped them out with all of the information and explanations.

They were so busy telling everyone else all of their knowledge that they almost forgot to hunt for their food, so they had to make some adjustments to their daily routine so they not only had time to pass on this new information to everyone but also the time that was needed to hunt and feed their families.

One and Another have kept their Time-stick in the hole in the flat rock at the top of the hill and they visit it frequently, just to see if the shadows make any changes to how it falls on the surface of the rock.

Over the many years that One and Another looked at the Time-stick, the shadows did not change from where they were marked on the rock with the hole in it, which held their Time-stick.

EPILOGUE

We've been together for a while now, as I've told you how hard Mother Nature has worked to bring her project of "Earth" to a point of some 3000 years ago.

Hopefully, Man has learned from Mother Nature and is prospering on the Lands of Earth and on the Oceans of Earth. It will be several thousand years before he begins to involve himself with the Air of Earth but that time will certainly come.

Mother Nature has been quite specific when She was instructing Man on how He should care for Her place called Earth.

Some of her mistakes are still evident to Man and he will soon learn to work with those situations as he is faced with them.

Mother Nature has shown all of her helpers and Man that with the respect that they now have for each other and the part which they all play to make her place called Earth the great place that it is, they need to continue to co-operate to keep everything in order.

Looking into the future, Mother Nature hopes that she is able to continue to encourage Man to follow her instruction on how to care for the place that She calls Earth, so that it will remain a thing of beauty, balance and prosperity for all who inhabit it. The Fishes that live in the Oceans of Earth, the Birds that live in the Air of Earth, the Animals and the Plants that live on the Lands of

Earth all must survive and co-inhabit the planet with Man. And Man must learn to balance what he takes from the Lands and the Oceans and the Air of Earth so they can all remain in the fine balance that Mother Nature has spent so many millennia to develop. She knows that if that fine balance that she has developed with the assistance of Sun, Weather, Moon, Seasons and her daughters Summer, Autumn, Winter and Spring is maintained, then everything will be as she wishes and everyone will survive and prosper. She knows that this balance can only be achieved if they all continue with their respectful co-operation.

But will it always be as Mother Nature intends?

Does Man continue to follow Her instruction? Or does he add more to the Earth, Oceans, and Sky than Mother Nature intended?

Only time will tell and Mother Nature keeps a close watch on how it all proceeds in Her special place that She has made, Her place called Earth.

ABOUT THE AUTHOR

David Kentish was raised on a dairy farm just south of Perth in Western Australia near the small settlement of Keysbrook.

Before the time of broadcast television, his father, J. Lance Kentish, spent time in the evenings inventing and telling stories about the Australian bush animals, the talking red-gum tree and the magic carpet to his family.

David has continued in this same vein with the telling of stories of imaginary Australian bush animals and friends.

He has completed two books of family history, *The Kentish's of Keysbrook* and, *The Kentish's of Keysbrook- The Next Generation*. These two books he has self-published and distributed amongst family and friends.

David has also completed an Australian adventure book, *King's Gold* that takes the reader through the outback of central Australia and into situations that are exciting and well beyond their control. This book has been self-published and is available in your local bookstore.

David and his wife Barbara enjoy travelling with their caravan in and around the Australian outback and bush. This is where he gets most of his inspiration which has led to a collection of stories of their travels. These stories form the *Travel Diaries Collection*. The collection currently consists of four books detailing their travels from 1999 to 2011. Look for these in the future.

Another booklet, *Beside the Billabong* is a story of Warragul, who is a juvenile Bunyip of Australian mythology and his animal friends who find the fun and adventures of living at a billabong.

The Fantastical Collection of Enlightening Short Stories was written whilst on one of these trips and is an intriguing story of how earth began and developed over many countless millennia. A well written story that will keep you intrigued right up to the last page.

David has several other works in the pipeline so keep a look out for more stories by David Kentish.

Here are some of what he has already completed:

Paperback
and E-book

Paperback
and E-book

Paperback
and E-book

Paperback
and E-book

Paperback
and E-book

Paperback
and E-book

Paperback
and E-book

Paperback
and E-book

DVD video

DVD video

DVD video

All of these and more at

https://www.davidkentish.com.au

Or contact the author,

david.j.kentish@gmail.com

Happy reading and enjoy everything that you do.

David Kentish

www.ingramcontent.com/pod-product-compliance
Lightning Source LLC
Chambersburg PA
CBHW050529280326
41933CB00011B/1512